Silver Burdett Ginn
MATHEMATICS
Exploring Your World

"Math by Me"

SILVER BURDETT GINN
MORRISTOWN, NJ ■ NEEDHAM, MA
Atlanta, GA ■ Deerfield, IL ■ Irving, TX ■ San Jose, CA

3 4 5 6 7 8 9-H-99 98 97 96 95 94

Contents

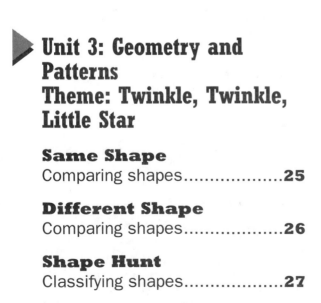

Unit 3: Geometry and Patterns
Theme: Twinkle, Twinkle, Little Star

Unit 10: Subtraction
Theme: Toys and Things That Go

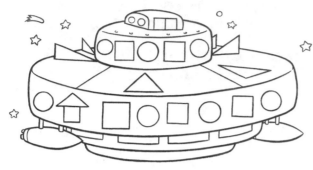

Unit 11: Numbers to 31
Theme: Sun Time, Fun Time

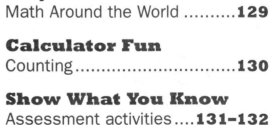

Ashanti Folktale

Draw a <u>under</u> the .

Draw a  <u>over</u> the .

Draw these things: .

Tell what they arc.

Calculator Fun

Use your calculator.
Press these numbers.
How do they look?
Draw lines to match.

PRESS	CALCULATOR NUMBERS

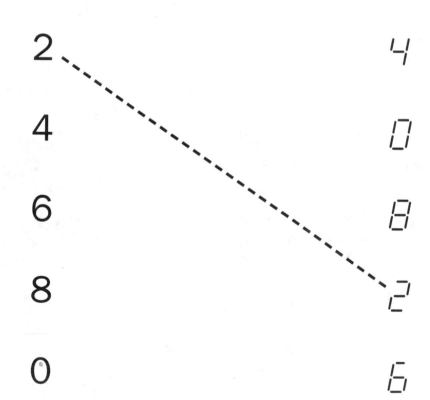

2   4

4   0

6   8

8   2

0   6

Name _____

Show What You Know

All Around the Town

Ring the man who is <u>up</u> and <u>right</u>.

Different

Draw one that is different.
Tell how it is different.

Tall Tower

Draw a tower that is taller.

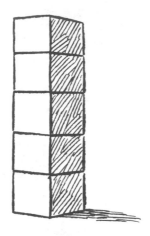

Building Tools

What shapes were used to build the house?
Ring them.
Tell how you know.

Name the Likeness

Ring a word to tell how
the shapes are alike.

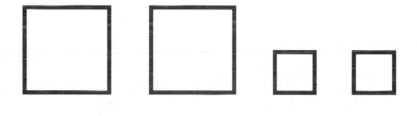

large   square

round   small

fat   sad

Think It Through • Journal Writing
Draw something that is round and small.
Then draw two more objects.
Make them like the first one.

Classifying objects   **seventeen** ⬦17

What Belongs?

Draw another one that belongs.

Think It Through • Journal Writing
Use your math journal.
Draw three objects that are alike.
Write how they are alike.

Classifying objects

The Inuit

Ring the ones that have the same use.
Tell why they belong together.

  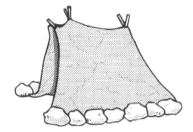

Think It Through • Journal Writing

Draw a playground in your math journal.
Think about what belongs at a playground.
Then add the objects to your drawing.

Name _____

Calculator Fun

Press each key shown below.
Ring the number that does not belong.

| ON/C | 1 | 1 | 1 | 1 | 2 |

| ON/C | 2 | 3 | 2 | 2 | 2 |

| ON/C | 1 | 7 | 7 | 7 | 7 |

| ON/C | 5 | 8 | 5 | 5 | 5 |

| ON/C | 6 | 6 | 6 | 9 | 6 |

Recognizing numbers

Name _____

What Shape Will It Make?

What shape will each spaceship
make when it lands?
Draw lines to match.

Think It Through • Journal Writing
Find objects in the classroom.
Use your math journal.
Draw the shape of the bottom of each.

Name _____

Is It a Bird?
Is It a Plane?

Which one will be a paper airplane?
Which one will be a bird?
Tell how you know.

Using a model

Circus Match

Draw lines to match one to one.

Think It Through • Journal Writing
Make drawings in your math journal.
Draw lines to match them one to one.

B Top Draw

D   group with more.

 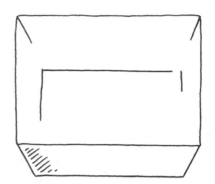

 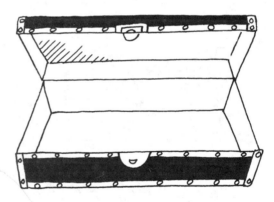

 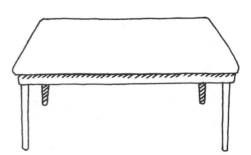

Think It Through • Journal Writing
Draw a group of clowns.
Then draw a group with more clowns.
Ring the group with more.
Tell how you know there are more.

Exploring same, more, and fewer

Name _____

Clowns, Clowns, Clowns

Ring the correct word.

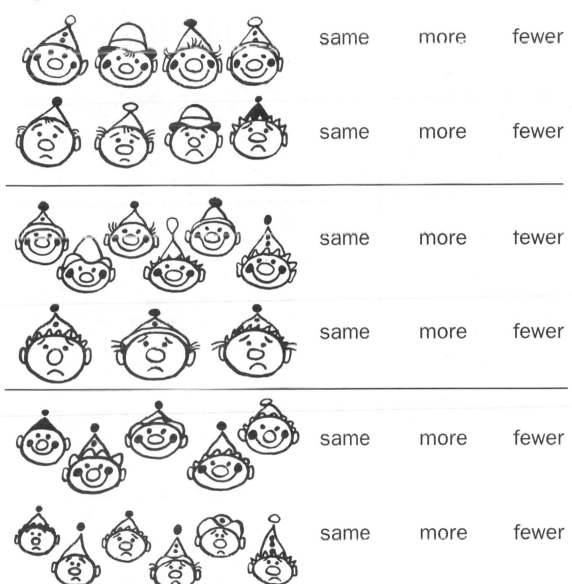

	same	more	fewer
	same	more	fewer
	same	more	fewer
	same	more	fewer
	same	more	fewer
	same	more	fewer

Think It Through •Journal Writing
Draw three groups of animals.
Make one group have more.
Make one group have fewer.
Ring the group that has fewer.

Color a Graph

For each  , color a box 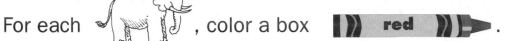 .

For each , color a box  .

Think It Through

Are there more or more ?

Tell how you know.

Building a graph to compare numbers

Circus Graph

Look at the graph.
Ring the answers.

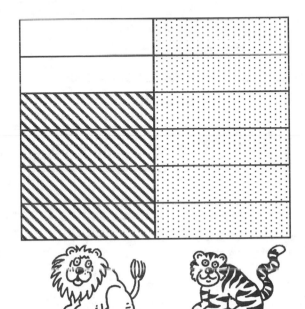

Which has more?

Which has fewer?

Think It Through • Journal Writing
Look at the graph.
Tell a story about what it shows.
Use words and drawings.

Interpreting a two-column bar graph

My Animal Graph

Choose 2 groups of animals.
Ring your choices.
Graph the numbers of the animals.
Color 1 box for each animal in the group.

Use [red] and [blue] .

Name _____

Two Rings

Make a big ring around the ones with  .

Make a big ring around the ones with  .

How many hats have  and ? _____

Circus Tents

Put an X on the one that is big <u>and</u> has  .

Ring the one that is small <u>and</u> has a  .

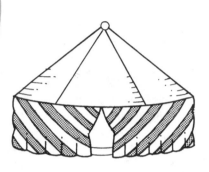
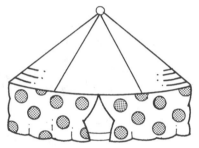

Think It Through • Journal Writing

Draw three tents in your math journal.

Make one with  and .

Make one with a  and  .

Make the other one different.

Comparing objects

Name _____

Kwanzaa Candles

Color.
Ring the ones that show the same number.

 red    black    green

Name _____

Calculator Fun

Press ON/C .

Then press ⎡ 1 ⎤ ⎡ + ⎤ for each clown.

Read the number on your calculator.

Write it.

Then press ON/C to start again.

⎡ 1 ⎤ ⎡ + ⎤ ⎡ 1 ⎤ ⎡ + ⎤ ⎡ 1 ⎤ ⎡ + ⎤   3 _____

⎡ 1 ⎤ ⎡ + ⎤ ⎡ 1 ⎤ ⎡ + ⎤ ⎡ 1 ⎤ ⎡ + ⎤ ⎡ 1 ⎤ ⎡ + ⎤ ⎡ 1 ⎤ ⎡ + ⎤   _____

⎡ 1 ⎤ ⎡ + ⎤ ⎡ 1 ⎤ ⎡ + ⎤   _____

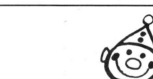  

⎡ 1 ⎤ ⎡ + ⎤ ⎡ 1 ⎤ ⎡ + ⎤ ⎡ 1 ⎤ ⎡ + ⎤ ⎡ 1 ⎤ ⎡ + ⎤   _____

Name _____

Kamba Finger Counting

Make the sign.
Write the number for each sign.

_____

_____

_____

_____

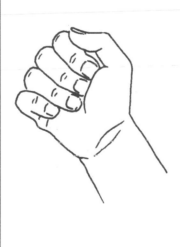

_____

_____

Name _____

Calculator Fun

Press ON/C .

Count the first row of pictures.

Press that number.

Then press ┌ + ┐ ┌ 1 ┐ ┌ = ┐ .

Write the number you see.

Press ON/C and start again.

 ┌ + ┐ ┌ 1 ┐ ┌ = ┐ _____

 ┌ + ┐ ┌ 1 ┐ ┌ = ┐ _____

 ┌ + ┐ ┌ 1 ┐ ┌ = ┐ _____

 ┌ + ┐ ┌ 1 ┐ ┌ = ┐ _____

One more

Ten Treasures

Count each row.
Draw more in each row to make 10.

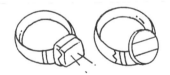

Think It Through • Journal Writing

Draw groups of treasure in your journal.
Make the groups in different amounts.
Make one group have 10.
Write the numbers next to each group.

Identifying numbers

Count Them Up

Count the fish.
Write the number.

_____ 7

_____

_____

_____

Think It Through • Journal Writing
Pick a number from 7 to 12.
Write the number in your math journal.
Then draw that number of fish.

Identifying numbers

Name _____

Ring 10

Ring 10.
Then write the number in all.

_____

_____

_____

_____

Think It Through • Journal Writing
Use your math journal.
Draw a large group of objects.
Count the objects.
How can finding 10 help you count?

Using logical reasoning

Five Are Inside

There are 5 mermaids inside the cave.
Write how many mermaids there are in all.

_____

_____

_____

_____

Spanish Numbers

Your teacher will say numbers in Spanish.
Listen for the numbers.
Put an X on the numbers that you hear.
Then color the circles.

Q	R	9	G	L	1	D	F	C
H	P	5	K	A	3	N	Y	X
L	D	7	C	M	2	Z	B	V
N	Y	1	2	3	4	3	K	O
V	C	X	Q	F	2	N	Z	W
X	A	Y	F	H	6	W	X	N
B	L	P	Q	S	J	K	L	A

What picture did you make?

_____

Calculator Fun

Look at the pictures of calculators.
Write the missing numbers on each one.
Use your calculator to help you.

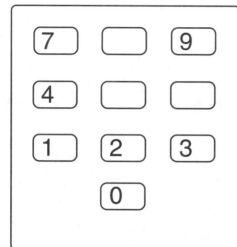

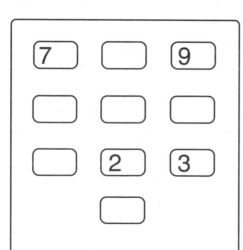

Hidden keys

Name _____

Show What You Know

Ring More

Ring the one with more.

Make Twelve

Draw more  .

Make each tank have 12.

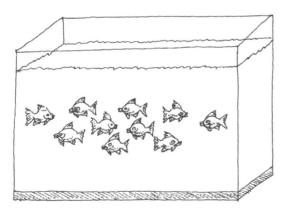
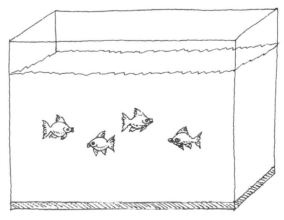

What's Missing?

Write the missing numbers.

3   4   5   6   ___

8   9   10   ___   12

10 and More

Ring 10.

Then write the number in all.

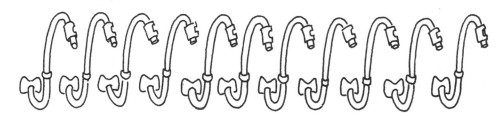

_____

_____

First, Next, Last

What happened first, next, and last?
Number each picture 1, 2, 3.

_1_   _3_   _2_

_____   _____   _____

Think It Through • Journal Writing

Think of a game you play.
Draw three pictures in your math journal.
Show what you do first, next, and last.

What Happens Next?

Look at the pictures.
Draw what happens next.

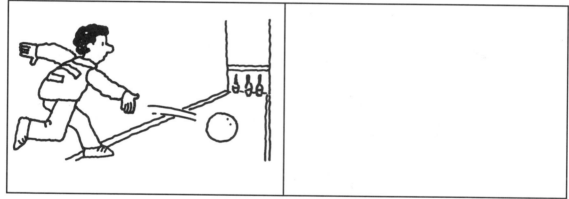

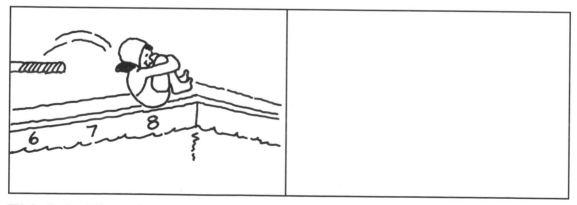

Think It Through • Journal Writing

What happens after you eat supper?
Make a drawing in your math journal.

Exploring sequence of events

Name _____

Trade for a Nickel

How many can you trade for a ?

Make an X on the pennies you can trade.

Think It Through • Journal Writing

Justin has a nickel.
You have pennies.
How many pennies will you give in trade?
Write the number in your math journal.
Draw the pennies.

Name _____

Price Tags

Count the money.
Write the price on the tag.

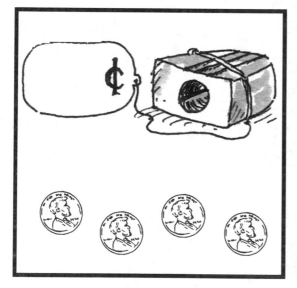

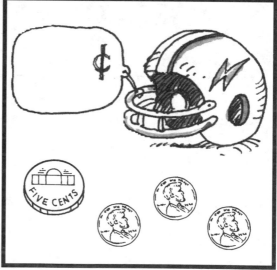

Think It Through • Journal Writing
Use your math journal.
Make a drawing of a toy.
Put a price tag on it.
Draw the coins that equal the price.

Values of pennies and nickels

Finding Dimes

Color only the dimes.
What do you see?

Think It Through • Journal Writing

Would you rather have a ![penny], a ![nickel, FIVE CENTS] or a ![dime]?

Tell why in your math journal.

Piggy Bank

Write a D on each dime.
Write an N on each nickel.
Write a P on each penny.

Count each kind of coin.
Fill in the table.

Dimes	Nickels	Pennies
_____	_____	_____

Name _____

Egyptian Water Clocks

Look at the water clocks.
How much time has passed?
Write the number.

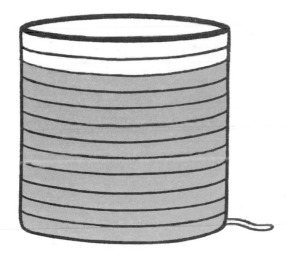

_____ parts of daylight
have passed.

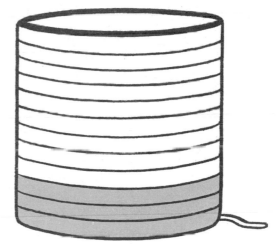

_____ parts of daylight
have passed.

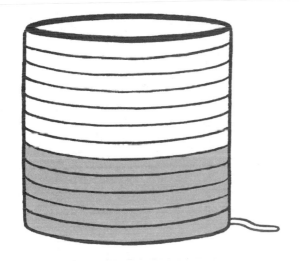

_____ parts of daylight
have passed.

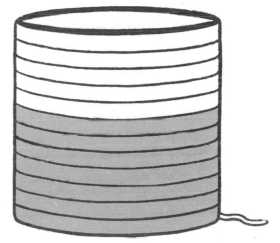

_____ parts of daylight
have passed.

Math Around the World

Name _____

Calculator Fun

Find the amount of money.
Color the key that shows the amount.
Press ON/C and the number key.
Write the display.

7 8 9
4 5 6
1 2 3
0

7	8	9
4	5	6
1	2	3
0

Counting coins

Show What You Know

First of All

What comes first, next, and last?
Number each picture 1, 2, or 3.

_____   _____   _____

Clock Time

Write the time shown on each clock.

_____ o'clock

_____ o'clock

_____ o'clock

_____ o'clock

Name _____

Coin Count

Count the money.
Write how much.

_____ ¢   _____ ¢

_____ ¢   _____ ¢

Make a Table

Look at the coins above.
Count the number of each coin.
Fill in the table.

Dimes	Nickels	Pennies
_____	_____	_____

Name _____

Tallest and Longest

Ring the tallest.

Ring the longest.

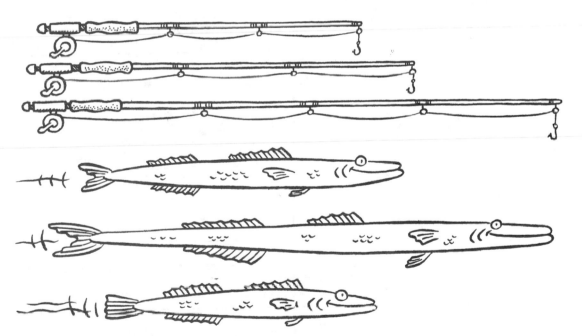

Think It Through • Journal Writing
Make a drawing of some friends.
Order them from shortest to tallest.
Make a drawing of some crayons.
Circle the one that is the longest.

Ordering objects by height and length

eighty-five ⟨85⟩

Draw a Shorter One

Look at the trees.
Draw one that is shorter.

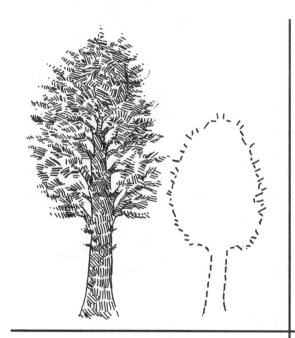

Comparing objects by height and length

Heavy and Light

Ring the one that is heavier.
Make an X on the one that is lighter.

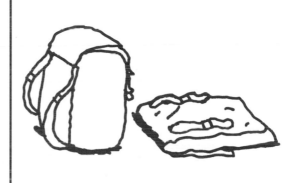

Name _____

What's on the Balance?

Look at the balances.
What might be missing?
Complete each picture.

Think It Through • Journal Writing
Use your math journal.

Draw two things that are heavier than .

Draw two things that are lighter than .

Comparing weights of objects

Name _____

How Much Does It Hold?

Ring the one that holds more.
Make an X on the one that holds less.

Name _____

Which Ones Can Hold It?

Look at the juice pitcher.

Which ones can hold all the juice?
Ring them.

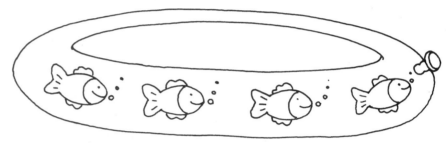

Think It Through • Journal Writing
What else can hold all the juice?
Make a drawing in your math journal.

Predicting capacity

Name _____

Equal Parts

Ring the ones that show equal parts.

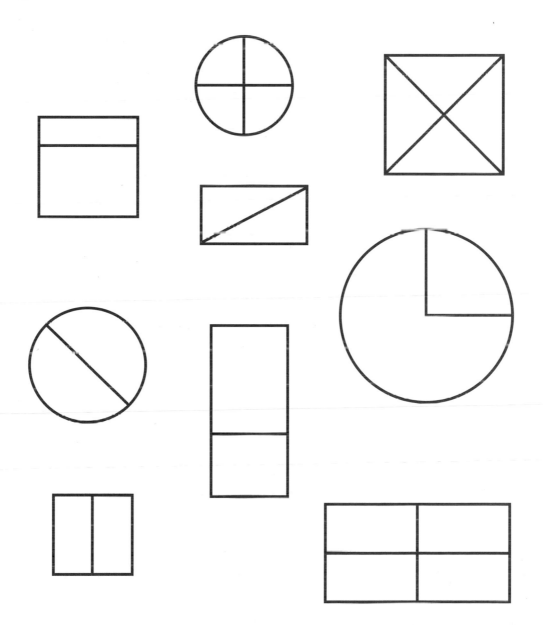

Think It Through • Journal Writing
Draw some shapes in your math journal.
Draw lines to show equal parts.

Measure It

Use some .

Measure each object.

Write how many  you used.

_____

_____

_____

Think It Through • Journal Writing

Use some .
Measure different objects.
Show your results in your math journal.

A Native American Game

Draw the Klamath sticks four times.
Change the order each time.

Name _____

Calculator Fun

Write the numbers.

Then use your .

Add the lengths.

Press

| ON/C | _____ | + | _____ | = | _____ |

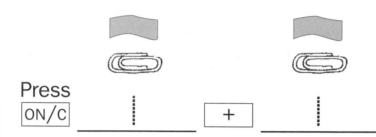

Press

| ON/C | _____ | + | _____ | = | _____ |

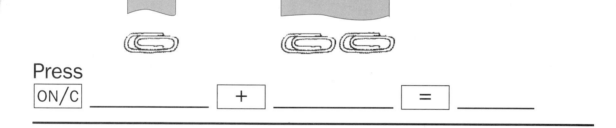

Press

| ON/C | _____ | + | _____ | = | _____ |

Show What You Know

Which Is the Longest?

Ring the longest.

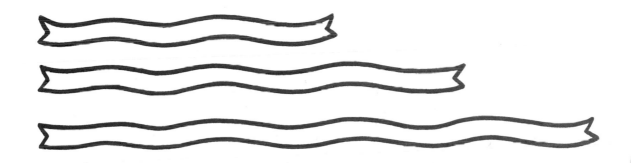

Which Balance Is Correct?

Ring the balance that is correct.

Name _____

Hold It!
Ring the one that holds more.

  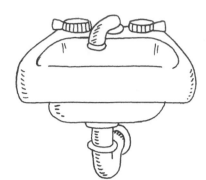 

Two Equal Parts
Ring the ones that show two equal parts.

  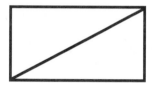

Cube Measure

Use .

Measure the .

Write how many you used.

 _____

Assessment activities

Name _____

1 More Animal

Draw 1 more.
Write the number in all.

 4

 ____

 ____

 ____

Think It Through • Journal Writing
Draw some sheep in your math journal.
Then add 1 more.
Write the number in all.

Adding 1 to a number

Tool Addition

Write how many you see.
Add. Write the number in all.

$1 \quad + \quad 1 \quad = \quad 2$

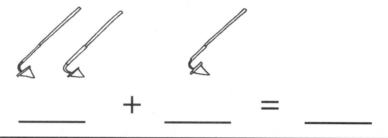

___ + ___ = ___

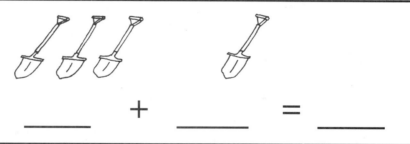

___ + ___ = ___

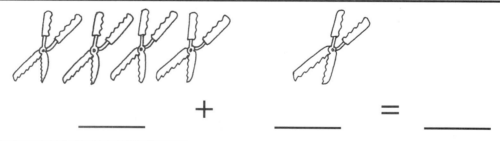

___ + ___ = ___

Think It Through • Journal Writing
What is + ?
What does it mean?
Talk about it.
Write about it in your math journal.

Adding 1 to a number

Seed Match

Look at the numbers of seeds.
Draw lines to match.

Think It Through • Journal Writing
Look at the numbers that are being added.
Write the numbers in your math journal.

Exploring adding down

ninety-nine ⟨99⟩

Name _____

Adding Bricks

Write how many you see.
Add.
Write the number in all.

$$\begin{array}{r} 4 \\ + 1 \\ \hline 5 \end{array}$$

$+$

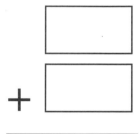

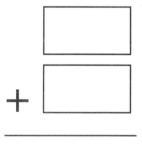

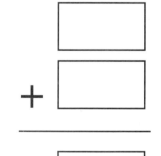

$+$

$+$

Adding down

Name _____

Garden Doubles

Ring the ones that show doubles.

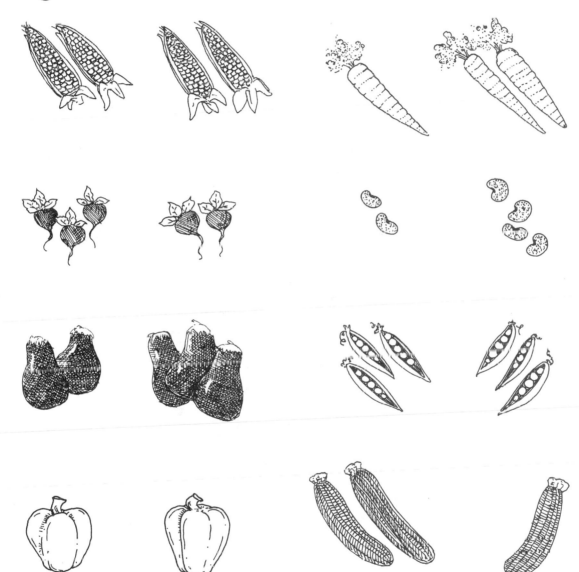

Think It Through • Journal Writing
Draw a double in your math journal.
Write the number in all.

Adding doubles

one hundred one 101

Adding Bean Doubles

Draw the number of beans.
Then write the number in all.

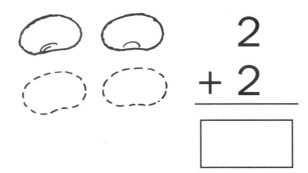

2
+ 2
☐

3
+ 3
☐

1
+ 1
☐

Think It Through • Journal Writing
Draw a bean double in your math journal.
Write the number sentence.

Five in All

Draw more .

Make 5 in all.

Think It Through • Journal Writing

How many hats did you draw each time?

Look for a pattern.

Write the addition sentences.

Name _____

Five Matchup

Look at the addition sentences.
Draw lines to match.

$$0 + 5 \qquad\qquad 3 + 2$$

$$1 + 4 \qquad\qquad 4 + 1$$

$$2 + 3 \qquad\qquad 5 + 0$$

Write the addition sentence that matches.

$$0 + 5 = \quad 5 \quad + \quad 0$$

$$1 + 4 = \underline{\quad\quad} + \underline{\quad\quad}$$

$$2 + 3 = \underline{\quad\quad} + \underline{\quad\quad}$$

$$5 + 0 = \underline{\quad\quad} + \underline{\quad\quad}$$

Addition patterns

Name _____

Using an Abacus

Write the numbers.
Use an abacus to add.

_____ + _____ = _____

_____ + _____ = _____

_____ + _____ = _____

_____ + _____ = _____

Calculator Fun

Add on your calculator.
Write the display.
Write the fact.

Press: | 3 | | + | | 2 | | = | | |

Fact: _____ + _____ = _____

Press: | 2 | | + | | 3 | | = | | |

Fact: _____ + _____ = _____

Press: | 4 | | + | | 2 | | = | | |

Fact: _____ + _____ = _____

Press: | 2 | | + | | 4 | | = | | |

Fact: _____ + _____ = _____

Adding on a calculator

Name _____

Show What You Know

Add 1
Write the number in all.

_____

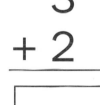 

_____

Add Down
Write the number in all.

$$\begin{array}{r} 3 \\ + 2 \\ \hline \end{array}$$

$$\begin{array}{r} 2 \\ + 3 \\ \hline \end{array}$$

$$\begin{array}{r} 3 \\ + 1 \\ \hline \end{array}$$

$$\begin{array}{r} 2 \\ + 1 \\ \hline \end{array}$$

Double Up
Ring the ones that show doubles.

Missing Numbers
Look for a pattern.
Write the missing numbers.

$$1 \ + \ 4 \ = \ 5$$

$$\underline{\hspace{2em}} \ + \ 3 \ = \ 5$$

$$3 \ + \ 2 \ = \ 5$$

$$4 \ + \ \underline{\hspace{2em}} \ = \ 5$$

One Fewer

Make an X on the last one.
Write the number that are left.

4

_____

_____

_____

Think It Through • Journal Writing
Use your math journal.
Draw some groups of toys.
Cover up one in each group.
Tell how many are left in each group.

Name _____

Subtract It

Write the number in all.
Write the number taken away.
Then write the number left.

$$\underline{3} \quad - \quad \underline{1} \quad = \quad \underline{2}$$

$$\underline{\hphantom{0}} \quad - \quad \underline{\hphantom{0}} \quad = \quad \underline{\hphantom{0}}$$

$$\underline{\hphantom{0}} \quad - \quad \underline{\hphantom{0}} \quad = \quad \underline{\hphantom{0}}$$

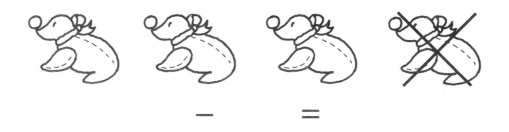

$$\underline{\hphantom{0}} \quad - \quad \underline{\hphantom{0}} \quad = \quad \underline{\hphantom{0}}$$

Think It Through • Journal Writing
What does – mean?
Talk about it.
Show your ideas in your math journal.

Subtracting one

Name _____

Nothing From Nothing

Look at the pictures.
Write the number left.

       4 – 0 = ____

      3 – 0 = ____

     2 – 0 = ____

    1 – 0 = ____

Think It Through • Journal Writing
Draw 5 toys in your math journal.
Subtract 0 toys.
How many are left?
What happens when you subtract 0?

Subtracting zero

Take Away Two

Tell how many are left.
Draw lines to match.

How many will be left?
Ring them.

Subtracting two

Subtraction Match

Match.
Draw lines.

Think It Through • Journal Writing
Draw six balls in your math journal.
Show some taken away.
Show your work in two ways.

Name _____

Subtract Down

Write the number in all.
Write the number taken away.
Then write the number left.

$$
\begin{array}{r}
4 \\
-\ 1 \\
\hline
3
\end{array}
$$

$-$ _____
_____

_____
$-$ _____
_____

_____
$-$ _____
_____

Share Your Toys

Use X's.
Make two equal groups of toys.
Then complete the number sentence.

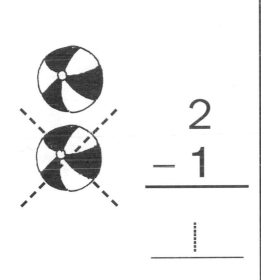

$$\begin{array}{r} 2 \\ -\ 1 \\ \hline 1 \end{array}$$

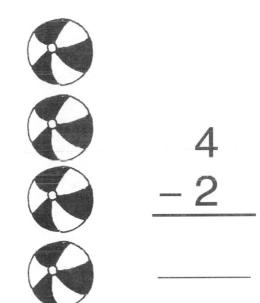

$$\begin{array}{r} 4 \\ -\ 2 \\ \hline \end{array}$$

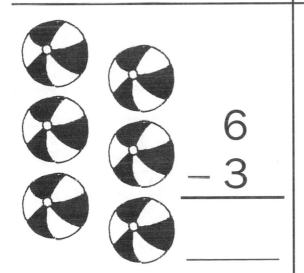

$$\begin{array}{r} 6 \\ -\ 3 \\ \hline \end{array}$$

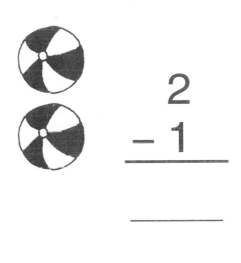

$$\begin{array}{r} 2 \\ -\ 1 \\ \hline \end{array}$$

Separating sets into equal parts

Add or Subtract

What does each picture show?

Ring **+** or **–** .

+

–

+

–

+

–

+

–

Think It Through • Journal Writing

Write a number story in your math journal.
Show your story with a drawing.
Write a + or – under your drawing.

Choosing the operation

Name _____

A Game from Israel

Play the game Good Shot!
Use the chart to keep score.

Player's Name	What's Your Score?
	6 − _____ = _____
	6 − _____ = _____
	6 − _____ = _____

Who had the least score?
Ring the winner's name.

Name _____

Calculator Fun

Subtract on your .

Write the display.
Then write the fact.

Press: [4] [–] [3] [=] [   ]

Fact: _____ – _____ = _____

Press: [6] [–] [2] [=] [   ]

Fact: _____ – _____ = _____

Press: [5] [–] [3] [=] [   ]

Fact: _____ – _____ = _____

Press: [6] [–] [1] [=] [   ]

Fact: _____ – _____ = _____

Subtracting on a calculator

Name _____

Show What You Know

Subtract One or Two
Write the number left.

_____

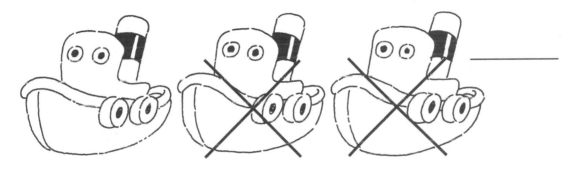

_____

Subtract Down
Write the number left.

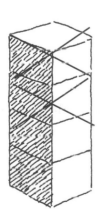
$$\begin{array}{r} 4 \\ -\ 2 \\ \hline \end{array}$$

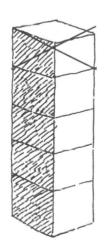
$$\begin{array}{r} 5 \\ -\ 1 \\ \hline \end{array}$$

Equal Parts

Ring the groups that show equal parts.

+ or -

Ring + or − .

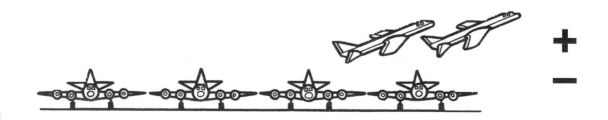

Name _____

More Fun in the Sun

Ring the groups with more.
Check by counting.

Think It Through
Was your first guess correct?
How can you tell which has more?

Estimating sizes of groups

Name _____

Sun, Moon, and Stars

Count.
Draw the same number.

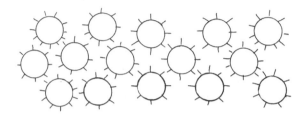

_____

_____

_____

Think It Through • Journal Writing
Draw a group of kites in your math journal.
Draw another group that shows more.
Ring the group that shows fewer kites.

Comparing groups

Name _____

Happy-Face Drawings

Read each number.
Draw that many 😊 .

┌─────────────────────────────────┐
│   │
│   **13**   │
│   │
│   │
│   │
│   │
└─────────────────────────────────┘

┌─────────────────────────────────┐
│   │
│   **20**   │
│   │
│   │
│   │
│   │
└─────────────────────────────────┘

┌─────────────────────────────────┐
│   │
│   **16**   │
│   │
│   │
│   │
│   │
└─────────────────────────────────┘

Name _____

In the Swim

Count.
Write the number in all.

_____

_____

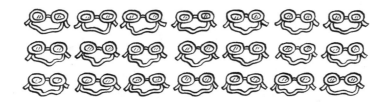

_____

Think It Through
How do you keep track as you count?
Talk it over.

124 **one hundred twenty-four**

Writing numerals

Name _____

Calendar Coloring

Color numbers greater than 28 |)) blue))|> .

Color numbers less than 5 |)) red))|> .

Color numbers greater than 18
but less than 26 |)) yellow))|> .

Sunday	Monday	Tuesday	Wednesday	Thursday	Friday	Saturday
				1	2	3
4	5	6	7	8	9	10
11	12	13	14	15	16	17
18	19	20	21	22	23	24
25	26	27	28	29	30	31

Comparing numbers

one hundred twenty-five 125

Missing Numbers

Write the missing numbers.

8	9	10	11	12	____
14	15	16	____	18	19
20	21	22	23	____	25
26	____	28	29	30	31

Think It Through • Journal Writing
Write a number in your math journal.
Write the number that comes before it.
Write the number that comes after it.
Which number is the greatest?
Ring it.

Name _____

Playtime

Ring 10.
Then write the number in all.

 _____

 _____

 _____

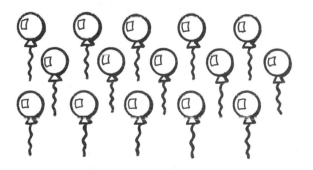  _____

Picnic Count

Estimate.
Ring your guess.
Then count.
Ring your answer.

ESTIMATE
more than 10
less than 10

ANSWER
more than 10
less than 10

ESTIMATE
more than 20
less than 20

ANSWER
more than 20
less than 20

Think It Through • Journal Writing
Draw many apples without counting.
Estimate how many.
Then count how many.
Were you close to your estimate?

Using logical reasoning

Name _____

Look at May on a calendar for this year.
Write numbers in the calendar below.
Make drawings for the different holidays.

May

Sunday	Monday	Tuesday	Wednesday	Thursday	Friday	Saturday

Name _____

Calculator Fun

Press each key shown.
Write each display.

ON/C | 6 | + | 1 | = | [   ] | = | [   ]

ON/C | 1 | 7 | + | 1 | = | [   ] | = | [   ]

ON/C | 1 | 2 | + | 1 | = | [   ] | = | [   ]

ON/C | 2 | 2 | + | 1 | = | [   ] | = | [   ]

ON/C | 2 | 7 | + | 1 | = | [   ] | = | [   ]

ON/C | 1 | 9 | + | 1 | = | [   ] | = | [   ]

◇130◇ **one hundred thirty**   Counting

Name _____

Show What You Know

More Ringing
Ring the one with more.

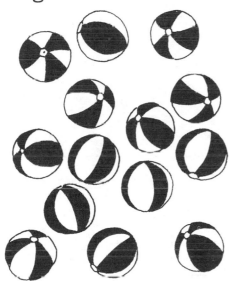
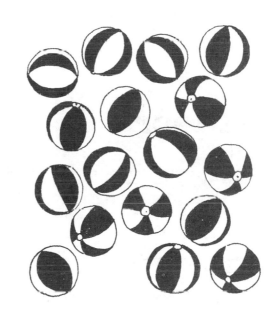

Stars and Suns
Count.
Write the number in all.

_____

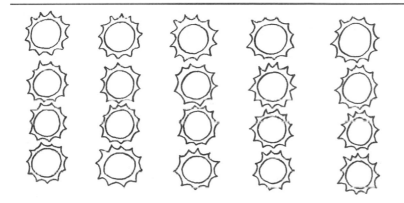
_____

Name _____

What's Next?
Write the number that comes next.

21 _____   14 _____

27 _____   30 _____

Outdoor Fun
Ring 10.
Then write the number in all.

_____

_____

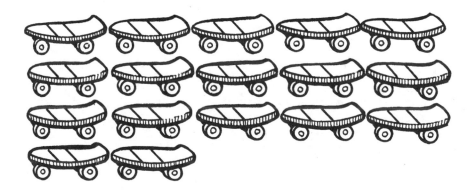

_____